TALKING
with YOUR KIDS
about JESUS

PARTICIPANT'S GUIDE

TALKING
with YOUR KIDS
about
Jesus

PARTICIPANT'S GUIDE

30 Conversations
Every Christian Parent
MUST HAVE

NATASHA CRAIN

BakerBooks
a division of Baker Publishing Group
Grand Rapids, Michigan

© 2021 by Natasha Crain

Published by Baker Books
a division of Baker Publishing Group
PO Box 6287, Grand Rapids, MI 49516-6287
www.bakerbooks.com

Printed in the United States of America

Library of Congress Cataloging-in-Publication Data
Names: Crain, Natasha, 1976– author.
Title: Talking with your kids about Jesus participant's guide : 30 conversations every Christian parent must have / Natasha Crain.
Description: Grand Rapids, MI : Baker Books, a division of Baker Publishing Group, [2021] | Includes bibliographical references.
Identifiers: LCCN 2021020361 | ISBN 9781540901002 (paperback) | ISBN 9781493428977 (ebook)
Subjects: LCSH: Jesus Christ—Person and offices—Study and teaching. | Christian education of children.
Classification: LCC BT203 .C7443 2021 | DDC 232—dc23
LC record available at https://lccn.loc.gov/2021020361

Published in association with the literary agency of Mark Sweeney & Associates, Naples, Florida.

Baker Publishing Group publications use paper produced from sustainable forestry practices and post-consumer waste whenever possible.

21   22   23   24   25   26   27   7   6   5   4   3   2

Contents

Introduction

When I speak at conferences and churches, I often begin by asking the audience two questions. First, I ask, "How many of you are here today already knowing that the world is becoming an increasingly secular place, and that it will likely challenge your kids' faith in some way?" Without fail, all hands go up. Second, I ask, "How many of you would then go to the next step of saying that you feel confident you know *specifically* what today's key faith challenges are, how to talk with your kids effectively about them, and what that means for you as a Christian parent on a day-to-day basis?"

Once in a while, a couple of isolated hands go up. But more often than not, the room goes silent without a single hand in the air.

I find this gap between knowing the world will challenge our kids' faith in Jesus and knowing what to do about it to be almost universal for Christian parents today. But it doesn't have to be that way.

My passion as a writer and speaker is to provide parents with resources that will give them the confidence they need to have the conversations that matter most. We don't need to be overwhelmed by the world; we just need to prioritize getting equipped to disciple our kids in an impactful way, given what they'll encounter.

In my book *Talking with Your Kids about Jesus*, I cover thirty of the most important conversations Christian parents should have with their kids today, given the challenges of a secular world. This curriculum is not designed to teach through *all* the subjects in the book. Rather, it's designed to walk you through an essential topic selected from each of the book's five parts: "The Identity of Jesus," "The Teachings of Jesus," "The Death of Jesus," "The Resurrection of Jesus," and "The Difference Jesus Makes." Session 1 kicks off these discussions with a conversation about overarching strategies for having meaningful faith conversations in your home.

My prayer is that this curriculum will ignite your passion for raising kids who are deeply grounded in God's Word and who will be prepared to stand strong as salt and light in a world that's increasingly hostile to truth (Matt. 5:13–16).

SESSION 1

The Art of
Family Faith
CONVERSATIONS

When I decided to start a Christian parenting blog in 2011, I had three kids who were ages three and under.[1] I thought I'd start a blog to connect with other Christian parents and share ideas for intentionally building a Christ-centered home. I had in mind topics like devotionals, fun worship songs, and ideas for developing a prayer life in my young kids.

That all changed a few months into blogging when skeptics of Christianity began to find my site and leave a steady stream of comments challenging everything I had to say. They made claims like "science disproves God," "there's no evidence that God exists," "the Bible is filled with errors and contradictions," and "Jesus never even existed." I had been a Christian my entire life but had never really engaged with direct claims against the truth of Christianity. I didn't know how to respond, and that's what started me on the journey to find and share answers to the many faith challenges today.

Looking back, many of the subjects covered in *Talking with Your Kids about Jesus* aren't ones I would have imagined having in the course of everyday conversations with my kids as they grew. (Basics of salvation? Yes. Whether God the Father is guilty of cosmic child abuse because Jesus died on the cross for us? Not so much.) In fact, if I had seen some of the chapter titles in the book, I would have been pretty overwhelmed! Perhaps this is how you feel too. But that's why it's so important to have a practical vision for how these conversations can look in your home. *Every parent can do this.* It just takes discipline and direction.

In this session, based on the introduction to *Talking with Your Kids about Jesus*, we'll talk about developing that vision through the idea of *low-grade tidying*.

Questions for Reflection and Discussion

1. Research consistently shows that at least 60 percent of kids who grow up in a Christian home walk away from Christianity by their early twenties, largely in response to intellectual challenges to their faith.[2] What are some of the greatest faith challenges you believe kids are facing today, based on your experience?

But How many return after twenty

Fit in , cultural appearance , World culture bombardment anti - christian message they don't know how to defend their faith

2. What do you think is the right relationship between parents and the church in equipping the next generation to encounter faith challenges? What role do you see as unique to each, and where do those roles overlap?

teach them how to pray, self supporting , involved or connected ,

12

how to mature in your faith and create disciples

3. What are some opportunities you see in your current family rhythms for doing "low-grade tidying" with faith conversations? Consider times when your kids are least distracted and most willing to engage (those times are different for every family!). It may be helpful to think back to meaningful conversations you've had in the past and what opportunities led to having those conversations.

Better about ready bible and Kids ready their own bible. they do find faith based teacher when they happen

— video

— Usny moments

— creating moments

Faith conversation

4. There are many kinds of barriers we might encounter when trying to initiate faith conversations in the home—our kids' perceived interest levels, busy family schedules, and our own feelings of inadequacy are just a few. What barriers have you personally encountered when trying to talk with your kids about Jesus? What are some ways you've been able to work through those barriers, if any?

— Scared to say wrong thing
— Do what I preach
  Hypocritical
—

5. In this session, we talked about the need to both "use" moments and "create" moments. When we use moments, we take advantage of times when opportunities naturally arise to bring up a related faith subject. What are some examples of times when you've used an everyday moment as an opportunity to talk about Jesus with your kids?

- I would like to do weekly studies with kids
- Nightly Bible ready
- putting a lens of Christiny on all thing we do

6. Looking back, what are some examples of times that you could have used as teachable moments but missed?

7. This session ended with the statement, "Homes where deep and meaningful faith conversations happen regularly aren't the product of lucky parents. They're the product of intentional parents who believe nothing is more important than raising kids to know and love Jesus." Do you feel your parenting currently reflects the priority of raising kids to know and love Jesus? Why or why not? If not, what changes do you need to make in order for that to be the case?

- Kids experience
and questions
    will be different
then ours

SESSION 2

The Identity of *Jesus*

Is Jesus God?

Throughout history, people have believed many different things about who Jesus was. For some, he was a good, moral teacher. For others, he was a failed Messiah, a mystic of some kind, or even a legend who never existed. For Christians, Jesus is no less than God himself—an extraordinary claim, to be sure!

Having grown up in a Christian home and church, I took Jesus's identity as God for granted for many years. As I share at the beginning of this session, that all changed when one day I picked up a book in the "Christian" section of a bookstore that presented a Jesus very different from the one I thought I knew. It's not that I didn't realize people had different beliefs about Jesus than I did. It's that I had never learned how to support my own beliefs with any kind of evidence. When confronted with someone *else's* evidence that Jesus *wasn't* God, I was left grasping for answers.

Our kids need to understand that knowing who Jesus is doesn't mean we blindly pick a belief from the many ideas that exist, but rather that we search for what is *true* of him. That search isn't very easy, however, in a confusing world. Our kids need intentional guidance. In this session, we'll learn a very helpful acronym that captures the breadth of evidence for what the Bible claims about the identity of Jesus. Later, in session 5, we'll add to this understanding with a look at how the historical evidence for the resurrection supports what the Bible claims. For more conversations on the identity of Jesus, I highly recommend reading chapters 2, 4, 5, and 6 in *Talking with Your Kids about Jesus* (content outside the scope of this curriculum).

Questions for Reflection and Discussion

1. What do you think is the most common belief that non-Christians have today about who Jesus is? Why do you think that belief is so common?

   Prophit , Good men,

   myth

2. What do you think are the most common barriers people have to believing that Jesus is God incarnate?

_____

_____

_____

_____

_____

_____

_____

_____

3. Have you ever struggled with believing that Jesus is God? If so, what were your own barriers to belief? If not, what has been the most significant reason why you came to believe that Jesus is, in fact, God in the flesh?

_____

_____

_____

_____

_____

_____

_____

_____

4. Which letters in the HANDS acronym[1] do you think offer the most compelling evidence that the biblical writers claimed Jesus is God and that Jesus *personally* claimed he is God?

_____

_____

_____

_____

_____

_____

_____

_____

5. Skeptics often like to say they don't care about a book written two thousand years ago or about a man who lived then. If your child asked why it matters what Jesus said and did so many years ago, what would you tell them? [Hint: Consider how this relates to Jesus's identity.]

_____

_____

_____

----

6. As parents, we often focus more on the teachings of Jesus than on his identity because we're preoccupied with the task of shaping our kids' behavior—we have many natural opportunities to share how Jesus taught us to live! It's not so natural for most parents, however, to raise the subject of who Jesus is and how we can *know* who he is. What are some opportunities you can identify in your family life to have more conversations around the subject of Jesus's identity?

----

7. In an online forum, a person asked, "Is there a [Christian] denomination I fit into or do I [have] to find another religion? I agree with everything except for the whole Jesus is God [thing]." Given what you learned in this session, what are some points you could share on how the Bible affirms that Jesus is God and how his identity as God is central to Christianity?[2]

SESSION 3

The Teachings of Jesus

What Did Jesus Say about Loving Others and Judging Others?

Part 2 of *Talking with Your Kids about Jesus* covers six subjects that both Christians and nonbelievers often misunderstand related to the teachings of Jesus. In this session, we'll focus specifically on the subjects of what Jesus taught about loving others and judging others (chapters 10 and 11 in the book). I selected these two subjects in particular for this curriculum because they're so frequently experienced by Christians, and they're often intertwined.

For example, one of the most popular articles I've ever written was titled "10 Signs the Christian Authors You're Following Are (Subtly) Teaching Unbiblical Ideas."[1] While it resonated with many—it's been shared over twenty-six thousand times as of this writing—I also received a stream of emails for months after it was published from people who wanted to let me know the Bible says not to judge. One person wrote:

> If "judge not, lest you be judged" is true, why is judging others a good thing? Not the ultimate sin, but it's a sin. How about the Great Commandment? Love God with all of you, and love your neighbor as yourself. What's not transparent about that? Jesus said it was the commandment to replace ALL OTHERS.[2]

This person's understanding of what the Bible says about judging and loving is common today: *You just said someone is wrong . . . Jesus said judging others is bad . . . You're the one who's wrong for saying someone else is wrong . . . and not only are you wrong, you're being unloving!* Of course, this puts the person in the ironic position of having made a judgment themselves (therefore making them unloving according to their own logic), but few stop to consider this.

In this session, we'll gain clarity on what Jesus actually said about loving others and judging others so we can more readily help our kids engage with these popular claims and misunderstandings.

Questions for Reflection and Discussion

1. What subjects related to what Jesus taught (or didn't teach) do you see or hear come up most often in our culture? (These could be on social media, in the news, in conversations with friends, or in any other area of everyday life.)

2. What are some of the key underlying reasons for the cultural disagreements you've seen or heard on Jesus's teachings?

_____

_____

_____

_____

_____

_____

_____

_____

3. *New York Times* bestselling author Rachel Hollis (a professing Christian) says in her popular book *Girl, Wash Your Face*: "Just because you believe it doesn't mean it's true for everyone. . . . Faith is one of the most abused instances of this. We decide that our religion is right; therefore, every other religion must be wrong. . . . I don't know the central tenet of your faith, but the central tenet of mine is 'love thy neighbor.'"[3] In this session, we talked about the fact that a biblical definition of love means loving God first, and when we love God first, we care for people's souls (as Jesus commanded). With that in mind, how would you respond to Hollis's quote?

_____

_____

_____

_____

_____

_____

_____

_____

_____

4. Popular singer Lana Del Rey has said, "When someone else's happiness is your happiness, that is love."[4] How would you explain to your child why this isn't consistent with a biblical definition of love?

_____

_____

_____

_____

_____

_____

_____

_____

_____

_____

_____

5. A very common claim today, especially among young people, is that Christians are too judgmental. If your child said this to you, what are some questions you could ask to clarify specifically what they mean by *judgmental*?

6. If by *judgmental* your child means that Christians call certain actions sinful, how would you respond?

7. A blogger wrote, "I think in general, we judge everyone way more than we should. Jesus never judged, He's always loved. If we're trying to live like Jesus, [then] loving is the best thing we can do."[5] How would you respond based on what you learned in this session?

SESSION 4

The Death
of Jesus

What Did It Accomplish?

A few months ago, I introduced my kids (ten-year-old twins and an eight-year-old) to the movie *The Sound of Music*. What I hadn't realized going into it was that there's a lot of background information that needs explaining in order for kids this age to have any idea of what's going on. We had to stop multiple times to discuss things like what exactly World War II was about, the relationship between Germany and Austria at that time, how Hitler could come to power, and why some people would be embarrassed by their kids playing in clothes made out of curtains.

Shortly after this, my daughter's second grade music class watched the movie at school. I laughed when she told me and asked how they did it without constantly stopping for explanations. She replied, "Oh, they all understood it. Well, kind of. I don't think they really understood what was going on, but they understood it in their own ways." I can only imagine what some of those interpretations of *The Sound of Music* must have been like! But no matter what any given second grader thought was going on, an objective reality exists. Someone may have thought World War II was a battle between unicorn armies, but the fact remains that it was something very different.

In the same way, Christians today sometimes reduce the significance of Jesus's death on the cross to whatever it means to them. They don't necessarily believe that his death had an objective meaning—a meaning that's true for all people. But the Bible tells us that Jesus's death indeed accomplished some very specific, objective things.

In this session, we'll start by looking at a major objection people have to the idea that Jesus died for our sins—one that kids are bound to hear today from both skeptics *and* some Christians. Then we'll talk about several important things that Jesus's death on the cross accomplished for us all.

Questions for Reflection and Discussion

1. Kids often hear the phrase *Jesus died for your sins* at church but don't always understand what that means at a deeper level. What do you think are some aspects of Jesus's death on the cross that are often not understood well by kids (or even adults!)?

_____

_____

_____

_____

_____

_____

_____

_____

_____

2. In this session, we heard the words of a progressive Christian pastor who feels that telling kids Jesus died for their sins can be psychologically damaging. Have you ever struggled with how

to present Jesus's death to your kids or others in a way that isn't troubling? Why or why not?

_____

_____

_____

_____

_____

_____

_____

_____

_____

3. We also heard the words of author William Paul Young who says that if God originated the cross, we worship a cosmic abuser. Using the framework we learned of Jesus's death being *planned*, *purposeful*, and *personal*, how would you respond to this claim? (Don't feel like you need to remember everything! Try to simply recall a key point from each of the three Ps.)

_____

_____

_____

_____

4. How does an accurate understanding of the Trinity also help us see why the "cosmic abuser" claim fails?

5. In order to understand what Jesus's death accomplished for us, we have to first understand the reality and severity of sin. If your child asked you what the big deal is about sin, what would you say?

6. To make *atonement* is to satisfy someone or something for an offense committed. As we talked about in this session, one of the most important things that Jesus accomplished on the cross was atoning for sin. What would you say to someone who claimed that Jesus should have just forgiven us *without* some kind of atonement?

7. How would you explain to your child why Jesus's sacrifice on the cross demonstrates God's love for us (John 3:16)?

SESSION 5

The Resurrection of *Jesus*

What's the Evidence?

The apostle Paul says in 1 Corinthians 15:14, "If Christ has not been raised, our preaching is useless and so is your faith." This is one of my favorite verses in the Bible because it's such a direct pointer to the ultimate truth test for Christianity: the resurrection. Paul is making it clear that if Jesus wasn't raised from the dead, we should pack our Christian bags and go home.

Kids today, however, will frequently hear that it's ridiculous to believe what the Bible says about Jesus being raised from the dead, and those challenges will come from all directions. Skeptics will claim that a resurrection isn't even possible and offer a variety of explanations for how Christianity otherwise got started. Even many *Christian churches* are now teaching that Jesus was only resurrected in some kind of metaphorical sense, despite the fact that the Bible clearly claims Jesus was *bodily* raised from the dead.[1]

In a world that considers belief in a supernatural event to be an embarrassment, we need to be very intentional in equipping our kids with an understanding of why there's good reason to believe Jesus was actually raised from the dead. In this session, we'll walk through the historical evidence for the resurrection, consider how popular resurrection theories fail to explain what we know, and gain clarity on why a supernatural resurrection is the *best* explanation for the historical data.

Questions for Reflection and Discussion

1. The apostle Paul gives us a very specific truth test for Christianity in 1 Corinthians 15:14: if Jesus wasn't raised from the dead, our faith is useless. People today often disregard Christianity, however, for all kinds of reasons other than that they've investigated the evidence for the resurrection and rejected it. What are some of the most common reasons you've seen or heard for people rejecting Christianity?

2. Is it important for you personally to know that there's historical evidence for the resurrection? Why or why not?

_____

_____

_____

_____

_____

_____

_____

_____

3. One of the four historical facts we talked about in this session is that the disciples believed Jesus arose and appeared to them after his death, as evidenced by the fact that they were willing to suffer and die to proclaim their message. How does this compare to others throughout history who have been willing to die for what they believed? [Hint: Consider what the disciples would have known firsthand versus what people like the 9/11 terrorists would have known firsthand.]

_____

_____

_____

4. In this session, we discussed the popular ideas that the disciples lied about the resurrection, that they were mistaken based on some kind of visionary experience, and that the resurrection was just a legend that developed over time. Which of these theories do you find least plausible as an explanation of the historical evidence? Why?

5. Which of the theories do you find most plausible? Why?

_____

_____

_____

_____

_____

_____

_____

_____

_____

6. If your child came home from school and said that their friend told them it's not possible that Jesus was resurrected because we know from science that dead people stay dead, how would you respond? What is the friend assuming?

_____

_____

_____

_____

_____

---

7. Bestselling atheist author Richard Dawkins was once asked what he thinks happened to the body of Jesus. Dawkins replied, "Presumably what happened to Jesus was what happens to all of us when we die. We decompose. Accounts of Jesus's resurrection and ascension are about as well-documented as Jack and the Beanstalk."[2] If your child read this and expressed concern that the evidence for the resurrection is comparable to that for a fairy tale, what would you share with them to help them understand the difference?

The Difference
Jesus MAKES

What Is a Christian?

For a long time, my son wanted a particular K'Nex roller coaster set, but it was expensive for what it was. Then one day I stumbled upon what I thought was the perfect solution: a K'Nex set with almost a thousand pieces that could be used to make a hundred different models! Instead of buying a single-use set for a roller coaster, I assumed this would be an opportunity to get him a set he could use to build a roller coaster plus many other things. I happily purchased it and gave it to him for his birthday.

A few weeks passed, and I noticed he hadn't built much with it—including a roller coaster. I asked him why. He replied, "The roller coaster? Oh, you can't make that with this set. It doesn't have all the pieces and connectors you need. You have to get the set specifically designed for that. Also, this set only came with detailed instructions for a few of the pictured models, so there's not a lot I know how to build."

I then realized the flaw in my logic. I had assumed that as long as he had hundreds of pieces to work with, he could build whatever he wanted, including specific designs like the roller coaster. But, as is obvious to me now, certain models need specific pieces that don't necessarily come in any other set—even one with hundreds of other pieces to choose from.

If we want our kids to build a robust understanding of Christianity—a specific "roller coaster"—we have to make sure they have the right pieces. A key purpose of the prior sessions (and of *Talking with Your Kids about Jesus* in general) has been to help you identify some pieces of understanding about Jesus that kids need today, given the difficult world in which they're growing up. But we can't stop there. Kids need guidance on how to put those pieces together accurately.

Without instructions, they can build *some*thing but not necessarily the *intended* thing. A distorted roller coaster isn't a big deal, but a distorted understanding of Christianity is. In this session, we'll focus on defining what it means to be a Christian and the implications this has for our understanding of God and the Bible.

Questions for Reflection and Discussion

1. How would you explain to your child what it means to be a Christian according to the Bible? (Use what you learned in this session to go beyond rather ambiguous definitions like "a follower of Jesus.")

_____

_____

_____

_____

_____

_____

_____

_____

2. How has your understanding of what it means to be a Christian changed over time, if at all? If your understanding has changed, what were some of the reasons for that change?

_____

_____

3. As Christian parents, we're in a unique position to make disciples of our children. What are some areas of discipleship you feel you've done well in? What are some areas you need to focus on more?

4. Someone shared on the Whisper app: "I'm a Christian, but I don't believe in the bible [*sic*]. I believe that there is a God, I just don't believe in a book written by man."[1] If your child said this, how would you help them understand the importance of the Bible for defining a Christian's beliefs and practices?

5. Even when we recognize the importance of the Bible, many Christians struggle to read it on a consistent basis. What barriers have you faced (or do you currently face) with reading God's Word regularly? What factors could help you get back into a better routine?

6. If your child told you that they believe the Bible is true and know it's important but find it too boring to read, what would you say? (This is a common feeling among kids!)

7. In response to an article about biblical morality, someone commented online, "Wow. Look how CERTAIN you all are. How SURE you are. You have convinced yourself that your understanding of God's love for humanity has been finalized. . . . Why not consider that others have experienced God in such a variety of ways that even if we wrote them in a book, they would only be scraping the surface to understanding God's love for us? Why not live out of a place of mystery—a place of love and acceptance of all people than live out of a place of all-knowing pride and righteous indignation?"[2] Using what you learned in this session (in particular, about the idea of putting "God in a box"), how would you respond?

Notes

Session 1 The Art of Family Faith Conversations

1. See www.natashacrain.com.

2. I discuss this in detail at Natasha Crain, "How Sunday Schools Are Raising the Next Generation of Secular Humanists," *Natasha Crain* (blog), January 7, 2019, https:/natashacrain.com/how-sunday-schools-are-raising-the-next-genera tion-of-secular-humanists/. For an excellent summary of studies, see J. Warner Wallace, "Are Young People Really Leaving Christianity?," Cold-Case Christian- ity, January 12, 2019, https://coldcasechristianity.com/writings/are-young-people -really-leaving-christianity/.

Session 2 The Identity of Jesus—Is Jesus God?

1. Robert M. Bowman Jr. and J. Ed Komoszewki, *Putting Jesus in His Place* (Grand Rapids: Kregel, 2007).

2. "Christians That Believe Jesus Is Not God (Me)," Christian Forums, October 7, 2003, https://www.christianforums.com/threads/christians-that-belive-jesus-is -not-god-me.61090/.

Session 3 The Teachings of Jesus—What Did Jesus Say about Loving Others and Judging Others?

1. Natasha Crain, "10 Signs the Christian Authors You're Following Are (Subtly) Teaching Unbiblical Ideas," *Natasha Crain* (blog), September 25, 2018, https:// natashacrain.com/10-signs-the-christian-authors-youre-following-are-subtly-teach ing-unbiblical-ideas/.

2. Natasha Crain, *Talking with Your Kids about Jesus: 30 Conversations Every Parent Must Have* (Grand Rapids: Baker, 2020), 117.

3. Rachel Hollis, *Girl, Wash Your Face* (Nashville: Thomas Nelson, 2018), 40.

4. It's not clear if this originated with Del Rey, but it's commonly attributed to her. See Lana Del Ray (@LDelRayQuote), Twitter, February 24, 2019, 3:16 p.m., https://twitter.com/LDelReyQuote/status/1099810264436887552.

5. Hannah K. Brinnier, "Hey Christians, Can We Please Stop Being So Judgmental?," Odyssey, July 3, 2017, https://www.theodysseyonline.com/christians -please-stop-being-judgmental.

Session 5 The Resurrection of Jesus—What's the Evidence?

1. For more on this, see chapter 19, "Why Does It Matter If Jesus Was Resurrected?," in Crain, *Talking with Your Kids about Jesus*, 194–201.

2. "Richard Dawkins: You Ask the Questions Special," Independent, December 4, 2006, https://www.independent.co.uk/news/people/profiles/richard-dawkins-you -ask-the-questions-special-427003.html.

Session 6 The Difference Jesus Makes—What Is a Christian?

1. "I'm a Christian, but I Don't Believe in the Bible," Whisper, accessed June 10, 2019, wis.pr/whisper/0518ad9d6fda11315345eb487bde84e787c1f9/Im -a-Christian-but-I-dont-believe-in-the-bible-I-believe-that-there.

2. Crain, *Talking with Your Kids about Jesus*, 265.

Natasha Crain is a national speaker, author, blogger, and podcaster who is passionate about equipping Christian parents to raise their kids with an understanding of how to make a case for and defend their faith in an increasingly secular world. In addition to *Talking with Your Kids about Jesus*, she has authored two other apologetics books for parents: *Keeping Your Kids on God's Side* and *Talking with Your Kids about God*. Natasha's articles have been featured in the *Focus on the Family* magazine and the *Christian Research Journal*, and she's been interviewed on radio shows across the country. She has an MBA from UCLA and a certificate in Christian apologetics from Biola University. A former marketing executive and adjunct professor, Natasha lives in Southern California with her husband and three children. She writes at www.natashacrain.com.

Connect with Natasha!

To read Natasha's blog and learn about additional resources for Christian parents, visit ChristianMomThoughts.com.

f @ChristianMomThoughts 🐦 @Natasha_Crain

EXPERIENCE THE
Full Curriculum

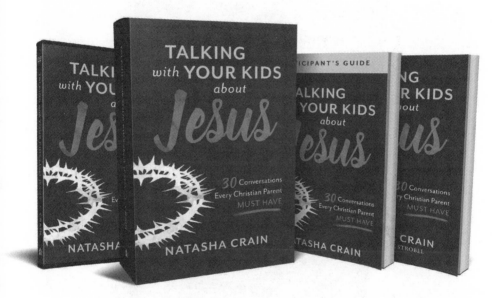

"Natasha is a trusted source for parents who want to provide their children with a vibrant and well-informed belief in Jesus."

—LEE STROBEL,

bestselling author of *The Case for Christ* and *The Case for Faith*

GET THE

companion book

TO *TALKING WITH YOUR KIDS ABOUT JESUS!*

Learn how to talk with your kids about the evidence for God's existence, the relationship between science and God, the nature of who God is, what it means to believe in God, and the difference God makes—all in the same parent-to-parent voice and accessible format as *Talking with Your Kids about Jesus*.